Contents

Meets **Accreditation Standard** for Child-created Bulletin Boards

Three Cheers for March PreK–K, SV 9840-X

Introduction

This series of monthly activity books is designed to give PreK and Kindergarten teachers a collection of hands-on activities and ideas for each month of the year. The activities are standards-based and reflect the philosophy that children learn best through play. The teacher can use these ideas to enhance the development of language and math skills, and of social/emotional and physical growth of children. The opportunity to promote pre-reading skills is present throughout the series and should be incorporated whenever possible.

Organization and Features

Each book consists of seven units:

Unit 1 provides reproducible pages and information for the month in general.
- a newsletter outline to promote parent communication
- a blank thematic border page
- a list of special days in the month
- calendar ideas to promote math skills
- a blank calendar grid that can also be used as an incentive chart

Units 2–6 include an array of activities for five **theme** topics. Each unit includes
- teacher information on the theme
- arts and crafts ideas
- a food activity
- poetry, songs, and books
- bulletin board ideas
- center activities correlated to specific learning standards

Implement the activities in a way that best meets the needs of individual children.

Unit 7 focuses on a well-known **children's author**. The unit includes
- a biography of the author
- activities based on a literature selection
- a list of books by the author
- reproducible bookmarks

In addition, each book contains
- reproducible **icons** suitable to use as labels for centers in the classroom. The icons coordinate with the centers in the book. They may also be used with a work assignment chart to aid in assigning children to centers.
- reproducible **student awards**
- **calendar day pattern** with suggested activities

Research Base

Howard Gardner's theory of multiple intelligences, or learning styles, validates teaching thematically and using a variety of approaches to help children learn. Providing a variety of experiences will assure that each child has an opportunity to learn in a comfortable way.

Following are the learning styles identified by Howard Gardner.
- **Verbal/Linguistic** learners need opportunities to read, listen, write, learn new words, and to tell stories.
- **Musical** learners enjoy music activities.
- **Logical/Mathematical** learners need opportunities to problem solve, count, measure, and do patterning activities.
- **Visual/Spatial** learners need opportunities to paint, draw, sculpt, and create art works.
- **Interpersonal** learners benefit from group discussions and group projects.
- **Intrapersonal** learners learn best in solitary activities, such as reading, writing in journals, and reflecting on information.
- **Naturalist** learners need opportunities to observe weather and nature and to take care of animals and plants.
- **Existential** learners can be fostered in the early years by asking children to think and respond, by discussions, and journal writing.

Gardner, H. (1994). *Frames of mind*. New York: Basic Books.

March News

Teacher:_____ Date:_____

Headline News

Coming Up

Happy Birthday to

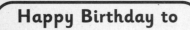

Special Thanks to

Help Wanted

Unit 1, Teacher Resources: Newsletter
Three Cheers for March PreK–K, SV 9840-X

March

Unit 1, Teacher Resources: Border Page

Three Cheers for March PreK–K, SV 9840-X

Special Days in March

National Nutrition Month   Have children celebrate with activities from the Eathing Healthy Foods unit that begins on page 71.

National Poetry Month   Read a poem each day during the month. Include familiar nursery rhymes that children can recite out loud.

1 Share a Smile Day   Have children cut out pictures from magazines of people smiling and make a smile collage.

2 Dr. Seuss's Birthday   Have children celebrate with activities from the Author Study unit that begins on page 86.

8 Aunt's Day   Tell children that their aunt is their mother's or father's sister. Have them make a special picture or card for a favorite aunt.

11 Ezra Jack Keats's Birthday Read *Peter's Chair* and discuss the character of Peter. Display other books by Keats that are about Peter and have children find him in each book.

11 Johnny Appleseed Day   Show children a picture of Johnny Appleseed and tell them his nickname. Challenge them to guess why he acquired that nickname. Then read a book about Johnny Appleseed.

14 National Preschooler's Day Plan a special snack in honor of preschoolers today.

16 National Quilt Day   Display a quilt and discuss with children the different patterns and shapes used to make the quilt. Then have them draw a picture on a square of white construction paper. Arrange and glue the squares on a large piece of craft paper to resemble a quilt.

18 First Walk in Space (1965) Display a picture of an astronaut walking in space. Soviet cosmonaut Alexei Leonov was the first person who walked in space. Discuss with children how he might have felt doing something that no one else had ever done before.

20 Bill Martin's Birthday   Display several Bill Martin books and read *Brown Bear, Brown Bear, What Do You See?* Have children make animal puppets and dramatize the story.

20 First Day of Spring   Have children draw a picture of how the trees looked in the winter. Then have them draw a picture of how the trees look in the spring. Discuss other changes that happen in the spring.

31 César Chávez Day   The founder of the United Farm Workers Association was born on this day. For more information on the life of César Chávez visit www.ufw.org/cecstory.htm.

March

Sunday	Monday	Tuesday	Wednesday	Thursday	Friday	Saturday

Unit 1, Teacher Resources: March Calendar
Three Cheers for March PreK–K, SV 9840-X

Calendar Activities for March

Classroom Calendar Setup

The use of the calendar in the classroom can provide children with daily practice in learning days, weeks, months, and years. As you plan the setup for your classroom, include enough space on the wall to staple a calendar grid labeled with the days of the week. Leave space above the grid for the name of the month and the year. Next to the calendar, staple twelve cards labeled with the months of the year and the number of days in each month. Leave these items on the wall all year. At the beginning of each month, start with the blank calendar grid. Do not staple anything on the grid that refers to the new month. Leave the days of the week and the year in place.

Introducing the Month of March

Before children arrive, gather all of the items that will go on the calendar for March. You may want to include the following:
- name of the month
- number cards
- name cards to indicate birthdays during the month
- picture cards that tell about special holidays or school events during the month
- a small treat to be taped on the day of each child's birthday. You may wish to gift wrap the treat.

Add a special pointer that can be used each day while doing calendar activities. See page 9 for directions on how to make a pointer. Place these items in a picnic basket. Select a puppet that can remain in the basket and come out only to bring items for each new month. A dog puppet works well because of the large mouth, which makes it easier to grasp each item.

On the first school day of the month, follow this procedure:

1. Place the picnic basket in front of the class. Pull out the puppet and introduce it to children if it is the first time they have seen it or ask them if they remember why the puppet is here. If this is the first time they have seen it, explain that the puppet will visit on the first day of each month to bring the new calendar items.

2. Have the puppet pull out the name of the month. According to the abilities of children, have them name the first letter in the name of the month, count the letters, or find the vowels. Staple the name of the month above the calendar.

3. Have the puppet pull out the new pointer for the teacher or the daily helper to use each day during calendar time.

4. Next, pull out the number cards for March. You may use plain number cards, cards made from the calendar day pattern on page 96, or seasonal die-cut shapes. By using two or three die-cut shapes, you can incorporate building patterns as part of your daily calendar routine. See page 9 for pattern ideas.

5. Place the number one card or die-cut under the day of the week on which March begins. Locate March on the month cards that are stapled next to your calendar. Have children tell how many days this month will have and

then count that many spaces on the calendar to indicate the end of the month. You may wish to place a small stop sign as a visual reminder of the end of the month. Save the remaining number cards or die-cut shapes and add one each day.

6. If there are any birthdays during March, have the puppet pull out of the basket the cards that have a birthday symbol with the child's name and birth date written on it. Count from the number 1 to find where to staple these as a visual reminder of each child's birthday. If you have included a wrapped treat for each child, tape it on the calendar on the correct day.

7. Finally, have the puppet bring out cards that have pictures of holidays or special happenings, such as field trips, picture day, or story time in the library. Staple the picture cards on the correct day on the calendar grid. You can use these to practice various counting skills such as counting how many days until a field trip, a birthday, or a holiday.

8. When the basket is empty, say goodbye to the puppet and return it to the picnic basket. Put the basket away until the next month. Children will look forward to the beginning of each month in order to see what items the puppet will bring for the class calendar.

Making a Shamrock Pointer

Include a shamrock pointer in the calendar basket for this month. To make a pointer, you will need the following:

- two 3" shamrock shapes cut from poster board
- a medium-sized dowel rod that is 18" long
- several 12" lengths of narrow green and yellow ribbon

Directions:

1. Hot-glue the ribbons to the end of the dowel rod so that they lie against the rod.
2. Hot-glue the two shamrock shapes to the end of the dowel rod so that the shamrocks cover the glued ends of the ribbons.

The calendar helper can use this to point to the day of the week, the number, the month, and the year as the class says the date each day.

Developing a Pattern

Practice patterning by writing the numbers 1–31 on die-cut shapes. You may want to use kite shapes in four different colors, such as green, yellow, orange, and purple. Write the numbers on the kite shapes in order using an ABCDABCD pattern. Have the children predict what color the kite will be on various days, such as the last day of the month.

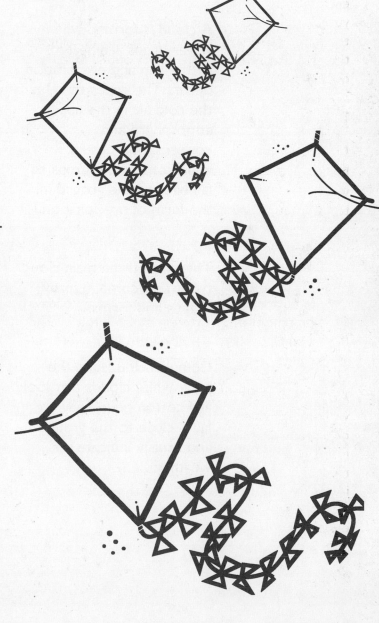

Three Cheers for March PreK–K, SV 9840-X

All Kinds of Weather

Weather on the planet Earth is affected by the rain cycle, which includes evaporation, condensation, and precipitation.

A cloud is formed when water drops are heated by the sun and evaporation occurs. The drops then hit the cold air in the upper atmosphere and condensation occurs, which causes the drops to fall back to the ground in the form of precipitation.

There are three main cloud types that come in many shapes and forms.

Cumulus clouds are the puffy white clouds that look like cotton puffs. They are fairly close to the ground and usually indicate fair weather.

Stratus clouds look like flat sheets of clouds and can indicate an overcast day or steady rain.

Cirrus clouds are high feathery clouds that are made up of ice particles. When scattered in a clear blue sky, they indicate fair weather.

Nimbus is a word often associated with clouds. *Nimbus* means precipitation is falling from the cloud.

Hurricanes and tornadoes are examples of severe storms that can form and bring strong winds and/or heavy rains.

Three Cheers for March PreK–K, SV 9840-X

Weather Mobile

Materials

- patterns on page 19
- white construction paper
- scissors
- glue
- hole punch
- yarn
- crayons or markers

Directions

Teacher Preparation: Duplicate on construction paper two copies of the sun, cloud, and raindrop patterns for each child.

1. Color the sun patterns yellow and the raindrop patterns blue. Cut out all of the pattern pieces.

2. Glue the two sun shapes back-to-back.

3. Punch a hole at the top of the sun and four holes across the bottom of the sun. Tie a desired length of yarn through each hole.

4. Punch a hole at the top of the two clouds and of the two raindrops. Tie these patterns to the four pieces of yarn at the bottom of the sun.

5. Hang the mobile from the ceiling.

Pretty Pinwheels

Materials

- pattern on page 20
- pencils with erasers
- pushpins
- crayons or markers
- scissors

Directions

Teacher Preparation: Duplicate a copy of the pinwheel pattern for each child.

1. Decorate the pinwheel pattern on the front and the back with crayons or markers.

2. Cut out the pinwheel.

3. Cut along each dashed line to create 4 sections.

4. Fold over each tip **A** to overlap **B** in the center.

5. Press the pushpin through the center of the pinwheel and into the eraser to attach the pinwheel to the pencil.

Scrumptious Sun Snack

You will need

- English muffins (one half per child)
- softened cream cheese
- pretzel sticks
- yellow food coloring
- raisins
- mixing bowl
- spoon
- paper plates
- craft sticks or plastic knives
- napkins

Directions

1. Mix a few drops of food coloring with the cream cheese until it turns yellow.

2. Place a small amount of cream cheese and a toasted muffin on a plate.

3. Spread cream cheese over the muffin with a craft stick or plastic knife.

4. Stick raisin eyes, nose, and mouth in the cream cheese.

5. Place pretzels around the edge of the muffin for rays of sunshine.

Note: Be aware of children who may be allergic to dairy products.

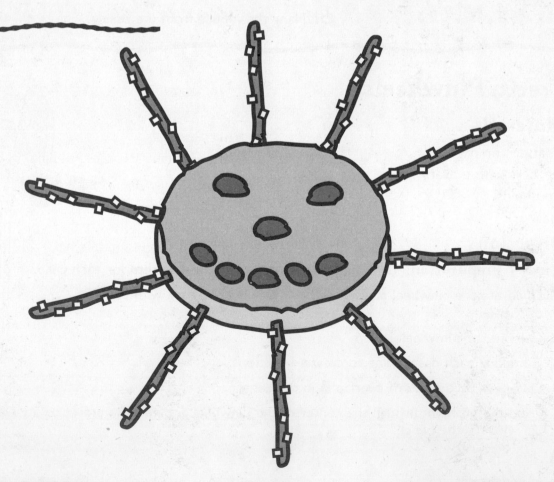

Three Cheers for March PreK–K, SV 9840-X

♫ Weather Song

(Tune: "Clementine")

What's the weather, what's the weather?

What's the weather like today?

Tell us, (child's name), what's the weather?

What's the weather like today?

Is it sunny, is it cloudy, is it rainy out today?

Is it snowy, is it windy, what's the weather like today?

Read About Weather in These Books

And Then It Rained . . .
by Crescent Dragonwagon (Atheneum)

Big Rain Coming
by Katrina Germein (Houghton Mifflin)

Cloudy with a Chance of Meatballs
by Judi Barrett (Atheneum)

Franklin and the Thunderstorm
by Paulette Bourgeois (Scholastic)

Gilberto and the Wind
by Marie Hall Ets (Puffin)

One Windy Wednesday
by Phyllis Root (Candlewick Press)

Rain
by Manya Stoijic (Crown Books for Young Readers)

The Cloud Book
by Tomie dePaola (Holiday House)

Stormy Weather

Materials

- pattern on page 21
- blue craft paper
- white craft paper
- yellow poster board
- scissors
- blue and gray tempera paints
- sponges
- paintbrush
- stapler

Directions

Teacher Preparation: Cover bulletin board with blue craft paper. Duplicate a copy of the raindrop pattern on white craft paper for each child. Draw and cut out a large cloud shape using the white craft paper. Draw and cut out a large bolt of lightning from the yellow poster board.

1. Read *The Cloud Book* by Tomie dePaola to children so that they learn about different types of clouds.

2. Cover the cloud shape with the children's handprints that have been painted with gray paint.

3. Have children cut out the raindrop pattern and use a sponge to paint it blue.

4. Staple the cloud, lightning bolt, and raindrops on the bulletin board.

5. Add a coordinating border and the caption.

Three Cheers for March PreK–K, SV 9840-X

Weather Centers

Art Center

Science Standard
Understands changes
in the sky

Rain Mural

Materials

- large piece of white craft paper
- food coloring
- newspaper
- masking tape
- spray bottles
- water

Teacher Preparation: Tape a large piece of craft paper on the floor for the mural and lay newspaper around the edges for excess spray. Fill spray bottles with water and add a few drops of food coloring to each bottle. Provide a bottle for each of the primary colors.

Have children stand on the edge of the mural and spray colored water into the air so that the mist will fall on the paper like rain. Have them use each of the primary colors. Hang the mural on the wall or cut it apart so that each child has a section to take home. Encourage children to talk about how the spray mist is like rain.

Math Center

Math Standard
Measures length using
nonstandard materials

Clouds Come in All Sizes

Materials

- pattern on page 22
- scissors
- white construction paper
- plastic snap-together blocks

Teacher Preparation: Duplicate five copies of the cloud pattern on construction paper. Enlarge or reduce each copy so that all five clouds are a different size.

Have children sequence the cloud patterns by size. Then have them determine the length of each cloud by laying plastic blocks from one side of the cloud to the other. Have them count the blocks on each cloud.

Weather Centers

Science Center

Rain in a Bag

Materials

- quart-size plastic bags (1 per child)
- measuring spoons, cups
- water in a plastic container
- one gallon-size plastic bag
- tape
- spoon
- potting soil
- fresh grass
- plastic tub

Teacher Preparation: Pour potting soil into the plastic tub and place the spoon in the tub. Place plastic bags, the container of water, the measuring cups, and measuring spoons on the table.

Take children outside to collect a handful of grass and place it in the large plastic bag. Add the bag to the science center. Have children scoop ½ cup of dirt into a small plastic bag and add one teaspoon of water. Then have them add a handful of grass and close. Tape the bags to a window that is exposed to the sun and leave for several days. Water drops will form on the sides of the bag when it is heated by the sun, which is like the evaporation stage of the rain cycle. The drops will then run down the sides of the bag to make the rain.

Writing Center

My Weather Pictionary

Materials

- activity master on page 23
- crayons or markers
- chart with weather symbols and words
- scissors
- pencils
- stapler

Teacher Preparation: Make a chart with weather symbols and words that correspond to the ones shown on the activity master. Display in the writing center. Provide a copy of the activity master for each child.

Have children cut the pages apart and staple them together in numerical order. Then have them trace each word and draw a picture to illustrate it.

Weather Centers

Language Center

Language Arts Standard
Identifies matching sounds

Letter-Sound Matching Game

Materials

- crayons or markers
- picture and letter cards on page 24
- blue and yellow construction paper
- glue
- scissors

Teacher Preparation: Duplicate the picture and letter cards. Color the pictures and cut all of the cards apart. Cut eight blue and eight yellow 3-inch squares of construction paper. Glue the picture cards to the blue squares and the letter cards to the yellow squares.

Have partners mix up the cards and lay them facedown on the table with two equal rows of blue cards and two equal rows of yellow cards. Then have them take turns turning over one blue and one yellow card at a time. If the beginning sound of the name of the picture matches the same sound as the letter shown, the child gets to keep the pair. If they do not match, the child turns the cards facedown and the partner takes a turn.

Dramatic Play Center

Social Studies Standard
Understands the importance of jobs

Let's Play Meteorologist

Materials

- laminated map of the United States
- 18" dowel rod or a pointer
- double-sided tape
- scissors
- markers
- unlined index cards

Teacher Preparation: Hang the map on the wall. Place the other materials on a table for the children to use.

Discuss how meteorologists use picture symbols to indicate the kind of weather each part of the United States is experiencing. Invite children to draw a weather symbol on an index card and cut it out. Use the double-sided tape to stick the card to the map. Then have children role-play a meteorologist by using the pointer and describing the weather.

Three Cheers for March PreK–K, SV 9840-X

Weather Centers

Block Center

Science Standard
Understands changes of objects in the sky

Structures and Shadows

Materials

- wooden unit blocks
- picture or drawing of the sun
- flashlight
- masking tape

Teacher Preparation: Tape the picture or drawing of the sun on the wall.

Take children outside on a sunny day during the morning and have them look at their shadow. Go out again in the afternoon and ask them if their shadow is the same. Discuss with children the movement of the sun and how it affects the length of their shadow. Invite them to build a structure using the blocks. Then have them shine the flashlight on the structure from different angles and notice how the shadows change.

Sensory Center

Science Standard
Understands objects in the sky

Sparkling Play Dough

Materials

- 1 cup flour
- 1 cup water
- 1 Tbsp. vegetable oil
- lemon extract
- orange pipe cleaners
- ½ cup salt
- 1 Tbsp. cream of tartar
- yellow food coloring
- clear glitter
- medium sauce pan
- spoon
- scissors

Teacher Preparation: Mix the flour, water, oil, salt, and cream of tartar with a few drops of yellow food coloring and lemon extract in a pan. Place the pan over low heat and stir until the mixture forms a ball. Remove from heat and place the dough on a flat surface. Knead in the desired amount of glitter. Store in an airtight container. Cut several pipe cleaners in half.

Have children make a play dough sun and add the pipe cleaners as shining rays. Challenge children to tell why the sun is important.

Sun, Cloud, and Raindrop Patterns

Use with "Weather Mobile" on page 11.

Three Cheers for March PreK–K, SV 9840-X

Pinwheel Pattern

Use with "Pretty Pinwheels" on page 11.

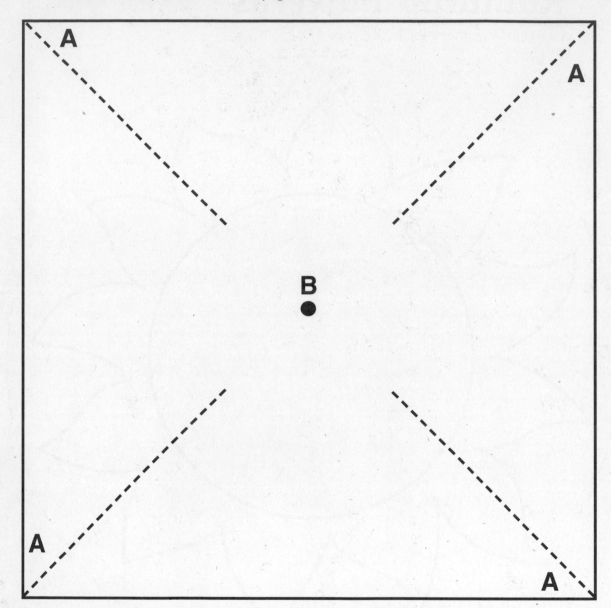

Bulletin Board Pattern

Use with "Stormy Weather" on page 14.

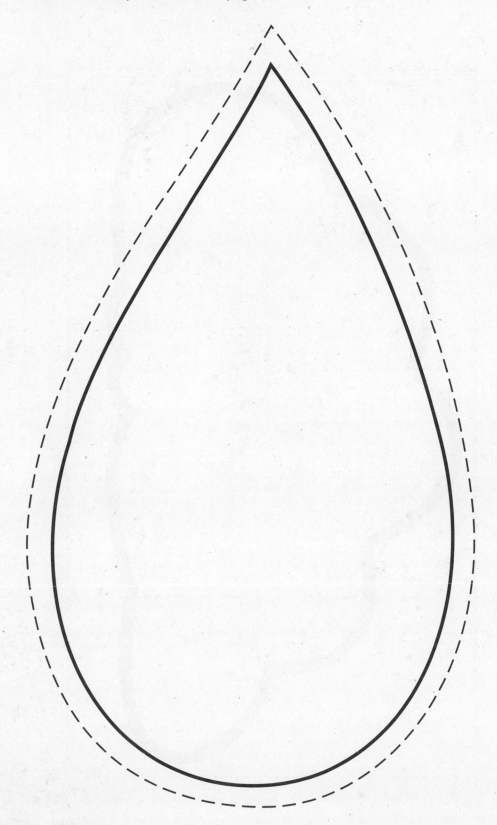

Cloud Pattern

Use with "Clouds Come in All Sizes" on page 15.

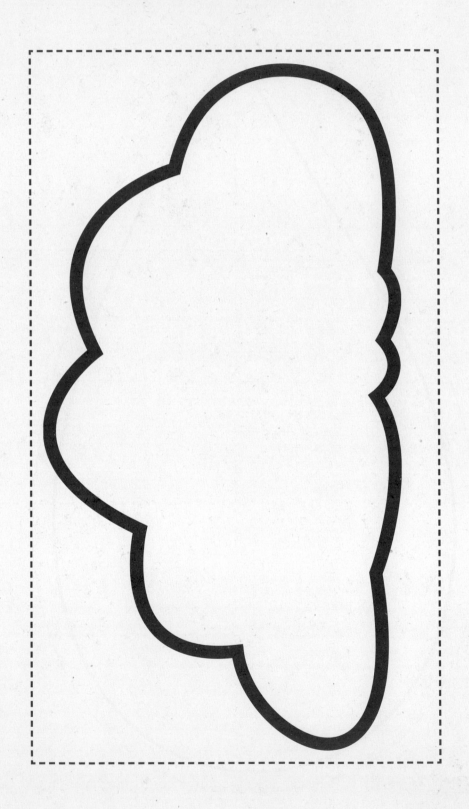

Three Cheers for March PreK–K, SV 9840-X

Name _____

Weather Pictionary

My
Weather
Pictionary
by
_____

sun

1

rain

2

cloud

3

snow

4

wind

5

Directions: Use with "My Weather Pictionary" on page 16. Have children cut the pages apart and staple them together in numerical order. Then have them trace each word and draw a picture to illustrate the word.

Unit 2, Weather: Activity Master
Three Cheers for March PreK–K, SV 9840-X

Picture and Letter Cards

Use with "Letter-Sound Matching Game" on page 17.

Rr	**Cc**	**Ss**	**Ss**
Rr	**Tt**	**Ll**	**Ww**

Three Cheers for March PreK–K, SV 9840-X

Pigs

 Pigs are excellent swimmers, and they prefer water to mud. They roll in mud to keep cool because they cannot sweat.

 Pigs are actually more intelligent than dogs and can learn their names by two or three weeks of age.

 A pig's sense of smell is very keen, and it uses its snout to root around in the dirt to find delicious tidbits like roots or fungus.

 Pigs form close bonds with each other. When they live in a group, adult pigs will leave their own litter to defend an endangered piglet.

 Pigs seek out and enjoy close contact with one another when resting. They can also learn to enjoy contact with humans.

 Pigs are vocal and communicate with one another frequently. Newborn piglets learn to come to the sound of their mother's voice. The mother "talks" to her young while nursing.

 A sow selects a clean, dry area apart from the group to give birth. She isolates her babies for five to ten days but then encourages them to socialize with the other pigs.

 The sow weans her young at three months of age. However, the piglets continue to live with their mother and other families. They seem to develop bonds with each other, and the piglets enjoy playing together.

Unit 3, Pigs: Teacher Information
Three Cheers for March PreK–K, SV 9840-X

Pig Puppet

Materials

- patterns on page 34
- brown lunch sacks
- pink construction paper
- large wiggly eyes
- pink pipe cleaners cut in half
- black crayons or markers
- scissors
- tape
- pencils
- glue

Directions

Teacher Preparation: Duplicate the patterns on pink construction paper and provide a copy of each for each child.

1. Cut out the pattern for the head, the snout, and the ears.

2. Glue the snout and wiggly eyes on the head.

3. Glue the ears to the back of the head and fold the ears forward.

4. Glue the head on the bottom flap of the sack.

5. Cut out a curved section from the open end of the sack to resemble legs. Cut out a small V-section for the hooves.

6. Color the hooves black.

7. Wrap a pipe cleaner around a pencil to form a spiral. Poke one end of the pipe cleaner into the back of the sack for a tail. Tape the pipe cleaner to the inside of the sack to secure it.

8. Use the puppet with the song on page 28.

Three Cheers for March PreK–K, SV 9840-X

Yummy Pig "Slop"

You will need

- one small box instant chocolate pudding per six children
- milk
- mixing bowl
- measuring cup
- whisk
- spatula
- mixing spoon
- raisins
- toasted whole grain oat cereal
- mini marshmallows
- chocolate chips
- one bowl per child
- plastic spoons

Directions

Teacher Preparation: Prepare pudding according to package directions. Stir in the remaining ingredients.

Discuss with children that sometimes farmers give their pigs leftover food and that it is called "slop." Pigs enjoy rooting out the tasty treats from the mud. Give each child a helping of the pudding mixture in a bowl and have them find the treats in their "slop."

Caution: Be aware of children who may have allergies to chocolate or dairy products.

Three Cheers for March PreK–K, SV 9840-X

♫ Old MacDonald Had a Pigpen

(Tune: "Old MacDonald Had a Farm")

Old MacDonald had a pigpen, e-i-e-i-o.

And in that pigpen he had a <u>pig</u>, e-i-e-i-o.

With a <u>wallow</u>, <u>wallow</u> here,

And a <u>wallow</u>, <u>wallow</u> there,

Here a <u>wallow</u>, there a <u>wallow</u>,

Everywhere a <u>wallow</u>, <u>wallow</u>.

Old MacDonald had a pigpen, e-i-e-i-o.

Replace underlined words with ones from the following categories.
Other Names for Pigs: sow, boar, piglet
Pig Verbs: squeal, snore, oink

Have children make the pig puppet on page 26 and sing the song with the puppet.

Perfect Pig Books

Olivia
by Ian Falconer (Atheneum)

Pigs Ahoy
by David M. McPhail (Puffin Books)

Pigs Aplenty, Pigs Galore
by David M. McPhail (Puffin Books)

Pigsty
by Mark Teague (Scholastic Books)

The Three Little Pigs
by Paul Galdone (Clarion Books)

The Three Little Pigs: An Old Story
by Margot Zemach (Sunburst)

The Three Little Wolves and the Big Bad Pig
by Eugene Trivizas and Helen Oxenbury (Aladdin Library)

Piglets in a Pigsty

Materials

- patterns on page 35
- white craft paper
- brown and pink tempera paints
- paintbrushes
- 6" and 9" thin paper plates
- pink pipe cleaners
- pink construction paper
- stapler
- scissors
- glue
- black markers

Directions

Teacher Preparation: Lay a piece of white craft paper the size of the bulletin board on the table or floor. Duplicate a copy of the ears, the snout, and the legs on pink construction paper for each child.

1. Paint ⅔ of the craft paper with brown tempera paint to resemble mud. Allow to dry and staple to the bulletin board.

2. Lay a small paper plate on a large one and position to resemble a head and a body. Staple the two plates together. Paint the plates with pink tempera paint and allow to dry.

3. Cut out all of the pieces. Glue the ears and the snout on the small paper plate and the legs to the bottom edge of the large plate.

4. Draw black eyes with the marker. Curl the pipe cleaner around the marker to resemble a spiral tail and staple to the large plate.

5. Staple the pigs to the "mud" section of the bulletin board.

Three Cheers for March PreK–K, SV 9840-X

Pig Centers

Math Center

Math Standard
Reads numbers to 10

Pennies in the Piggy Bank

Materials

- patterns on page 36
- markers or crayons
- 80 pennies
- container to hold pennies
- scissors
- file folder
- glue

Teacher Preparation: Duplicate ten copies of the pig pattern. Color and cut out the pigs. Arrange and glue the pigs on the inside of the file folder in a pleasing arrangement. Write a number from 1–10 on each of the pigs.

Have children count out the number of pennies indicated on each of the pigs and place them on the correct pig.

Block Center

Math Standard
Uses familiar manipulatives to recognize shapes and their relationships

Old MacDonald Had a Pigsty

Materials

- wooden unit blocks
- a small shoe box
- brown tissue paper
- pictures of pigs in mud
- toy pigs

Teacher Preparation: Display the pictures in the block center.

Discuss with children the meaning of a pigsty and how pigs roll in mud to cool their bodies. Pigs cannot sweat when they get hot. Have children build a fence with the blocks and place the shoe box inside the fence for the food trough. Then have them tear the brown tissue paper into pieces and crumple them up. Throw the crumpled pieces inside the fenced area to represent mud and add the toy pigs.

Tip: Invite children to bring a stuffed toy pig from home to add to the center.

Pig Centers

Reading Center

Retelling "The Three Little Pigs"

Materials

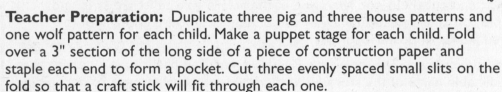

- version of *The Three Little Pigs*
- 9" x 12" construction paper
- glue
- craft sticks (4 per child)
- straw
- ½" x 1" red construction paper rectangles
- patterns on page 36
- scissors
- crayons
- stapler
- toothpicks

Teacher Preparation: Duplicate three pig and three house patterns and one wolf pattern for each child. Make a puppet stage for each child. Fold over a 3" section of the long side of a piece of construction paper and staple each end to form a pocket. Cut three evenly spaced small slits on the fold so that a craft stick will fit through each one.

Read the story of *The Three Little Pigs*. Have children participate by saying the predictable parts of the story. Then have them color the wolf and each of the three pigs a different color and cut them out. Tell children to glue each pig and the wolf to a craft stick. Have them cut out the three houses and glue each house above the folded section of the puppet stage. Have children place one house above each slit. Then have them glue a small amount of straw on the first house, several toothpicks on the second house, and several red "bricks" on the third house. Tell children to insert one pig puppet in each of the three slits so that the stick hangs free and the face is hidden in the pocket.

Have children retell the story by pushing one pig puppet up at a time so that he is in front of his house. Have them hide the pig when the wolf blows the house down.

Pig Centers

Dramatic Play Center

Language Arts Standard
Sequences events accurately

Little Pig, Let Me Come In

Materials

- patterns on pages 37 and 38
- sentence strips
- masking tape
- scissors
- 3 pieces of white poster board
- version of *The Three Little Pigs*
- crayons or markers
- glue
- stapler

Teacher Preparation: Duplicate three pig patterns and one wolf pattern. Color and cut them out. Then glue each pattern to a sentence strip and staple to make a headband. Draw the outline of a house on each of the three pieces of poster board.

Read the story of *The Three Little Pigs*. Have children participate by saying the predictable parts of the story. Have them work in small groups to decorate the three houses according to the story. Hang the three houses on the wall in the dramatic play center. Encourage children to role-play the story using the headbands and the houses.

Language Center

Language Arts Standard
Identifies medial sounds

Pink Pig Puzzle

Materials

- activity master on page 39
- pink and blue crayons

Teacher Preparation: Duplicate a copy of the activity master for each child.

Have children use a pink crayon to color the spaces that show pictures whose names have the medial *i* sound like *pig*. Tell them to color all of the other spaces blue. For younger children white out the pictures and write letters of the alphabet in each section. Use capital and lowercase letters *Pp* for them to color pink and various other letters to color blue.

Pig Centers

Sensory Center

Science Standard
Understands characteristics of organisms

Rooting in the Mud

Materials

- plastic tub
- paint aprons or shirts
- dirt
- water
- collection of small objects such as plastic animals, marbles, smooth rocks, or keys

Teacher Preparation: Pour dirt into the plastic tub and add water until a smooth consistency of mud is formed. Hide small objects in the mud.

Discuss with children that pigs have a keen sense of smell and use their snouts to root up tasty morsels in dirt or mud. Have children wear aprons or paint shirts to cover clothing. Invite them to use their hands to root out as many objects as they can from the mud.

Tip: Cover the table or floor with an old shower curtain for easy cleanup. Place this center near a sink or have a tub of water nearby for children to wash their hands.

Writing Center

Language Arts Standard
Writes words from left to right

Describing Pigs

Materials

- activity master on page 40
- several pictures of pigs
- pencils
- crayons

Teacher Preparation: Duplicate a copy of the activity master for each child.

Discuss with children words that describe. Display several pictures of pigs and have them describe the pigs. Then have them draw a picture of a pig and write or dictate two words that describe their pig.

Sack Puppet Patterns

Use with "Pig Puppet" on page 26.

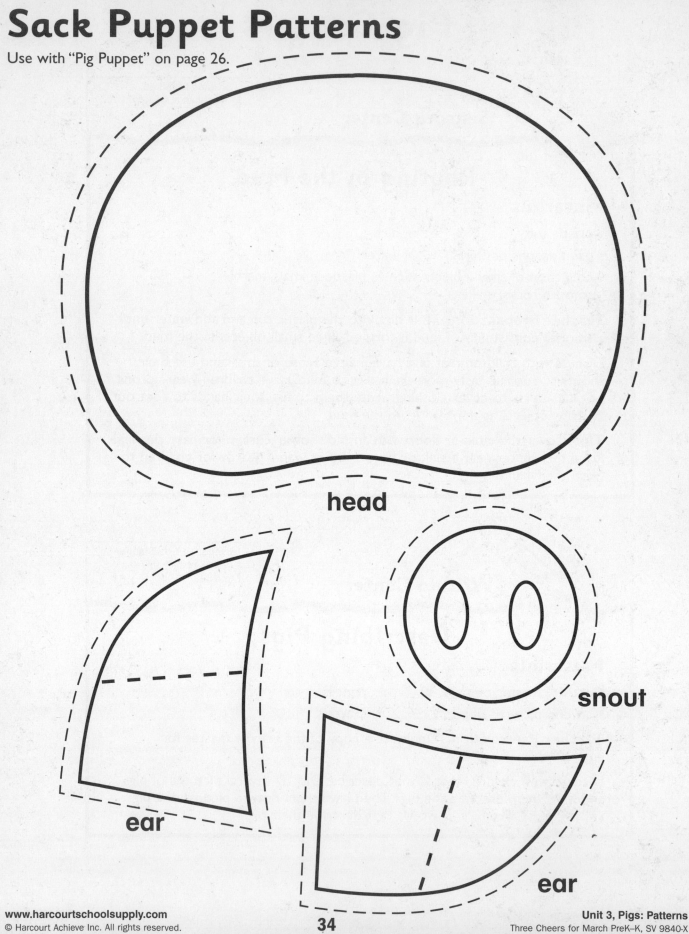

head

snout

ear

ear

Three Cheers for March PreK–K, SV 9840-X

Pig Patterns

Use with "Piglets in a Pigsty" on page 29.

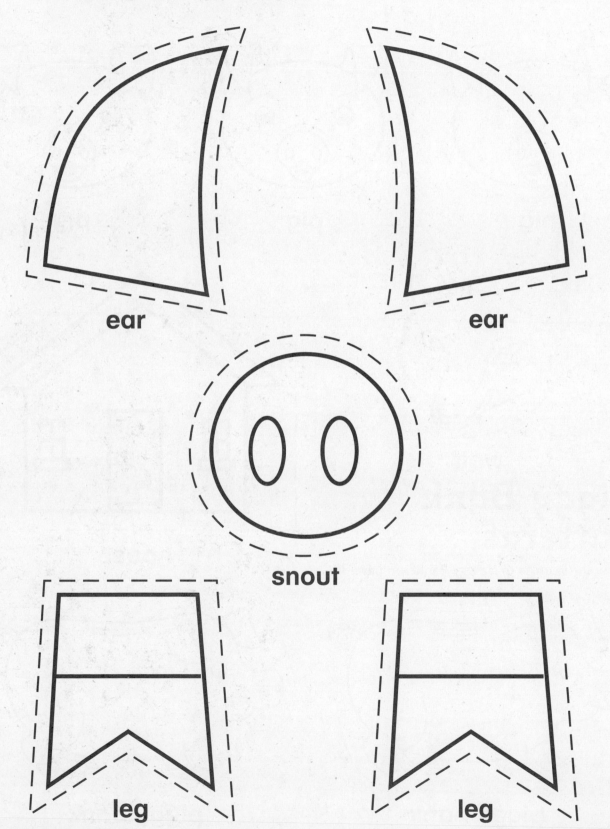

ear   ear

snout

leg   leg

Three Cheers for March PreK–K, SV 9840-X

Puppet Patterns

Use with "Retelling 'The Three Little Pigs'" on page 31.

pig

pig

pig

wolf

Piggy Bank Patterns

Use with "Pennies in a Piggy Bank" on page 30.

house

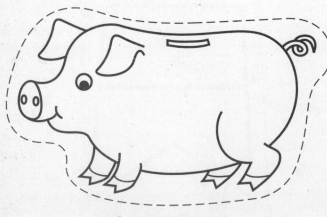

piggy bank

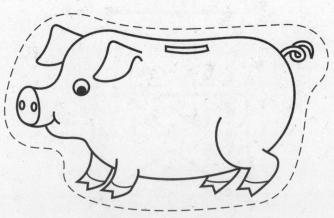

piggy bank

Pig Headband

Use with "Little Pig, Let Me Come In" on page 32.

Wolf Headband

Use with "Little Pig, Let Me Come In" on page 32.

Unit 3, Pigs: Pattern
Three Cheers for March PreK–K, SV 9840-X

Name _____

Puzzle Fun

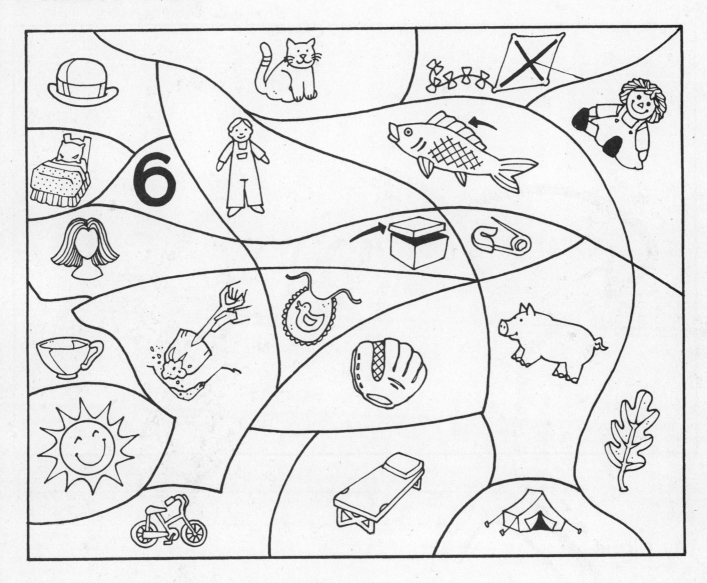

Directions: Use with "Pink Pig Puzzle" on page 32. Have children use a pink crayon to color the spaces that show pictures whose names have the medial *i* sound like *pig*. Tell them to color all of the other spaces blue.

Unit 3, Pigs: Activity Master
Three Cheers for March PreK–K, SV 9840-X

Name _____

Writing Fun

My pig is _____.

My pig is _____.

I like pigs.

Directions: Use with "Describing Pigs" on page 33. Have children draw a picture of a pig and write or dictate two words that describe their pig.

Saint Patrick's Day and the Leprechauns

 Saint Patrick's Day is celebrated each year on March 17.

 It is both a holy day and a national holiday in Ireland. Saint Patrick is the patron saint who brought Christianity to the Irish.

 Legend says that Saint Patrick used a shamrock, which has three leaves, to tell about the Trinity (God as the Father, the Son, and the Holy Spirit).

 People all around the world celebrate Saint Patrick's Day by wearing green, which is reminiscent of the beautiful green countryside of Ireland. Many cities celebrate the day with a parade.

 Another legend about Saint Patrick is that he drove the snakes from Ireland. It is true that there are no snakes in Ireland. However, it is because a cold-blooded animal like a snake cannot survive the freezing temperatures of the region.

 The leprechaun is a fairy-like, solitary creature that is also associated with Ireland and Saint Patrick's Day.

 The story of the leprechaun says that they are small men who must guard the treasures of the other fairies. There are no female leprechauns.

 No matter how hard a leprechaun tries to hide the gold, the presence of a rainbow alerts mortals to the whereabouts of the treasure. Thus, the rainbow has become associated with leprechauns.

 It is also said that if a mortal catches a leprechaun and demands the treasure, the leprechaun will give it to the mortal. What an exciting story to pass from generation to generation!

Wearing of the Green

Materials

- pattern on page 50
- green construction paper
- 6" lengths of green curly ribbon (3 per child)
- green glitter
- green pony beads
- yarn
- glue
- scissors
- stapler
- tape
- hole punch

Directions

Teacher Preparation: Duplicate the shamrock pattern on green construction paper. Provide a shamrock for each child. Tie a knot at one end of each length of ribbon.

1. Cut out the shamrock.

2. Decorate the shamrock using the glue and the glitter. Allow to dry.

3. String a few beads on each of the three lengths of ribbon that have knots on the ends.

4. Staple or tape the ribbons to the back of the shamrock so that they hang freely.

5. Punch two holes at the top of the shamrock and string yarn through the holes.

6. Tie the two ends together and wear as a necklace on Saint Patrick's Day.

Rainbow Streamers

Materials

- 9" thin paper plates (one per child)
- scissors
- rolls of purple, blue, green, yellow, orange, and red crepe paper streamers
- stapler or glue
- yardstick
- picture of a rainbow

Directions

Teacher Preparation: Cut 2' to 3' streamers of each color for younger children.

Display a picture of a rainbow and have children name the colors they see in it. Then discuss with them the legend of the leprechaun's pot of gold at the end of the rainbow.

1. Use the yardstick to measure and use scissors to cut a 2' to 3' streamer from each of the six rainbow colors.

2. Staple or glue the streamers in rainbow sequence on the edge of a paper plate so that they hang freely.

3. Fold the plate in half, covering the edges of the streamers, and staple the plate's edges together.

4. Cut a rectangle through both thicknesses near the folded edge of the plate for a handle.

5. Run outside with your rainbow streamers!

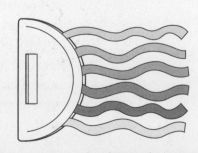

Three Cheers for March PreK–K, SV 9840-X

Green Treats

You will need

- one plain sugar cookie per child
- white frosting
- green food coloring
- rainbow sprinkles
- milk (one cup per child)
- 8-ounce clear plastic cups
- green straws
- green napkins
- craft sticks or plastic knives

Directions

1. Stir in several drops of food coloring with frosting and mix until it turns green.

2. Put a small amount of frosting on each cookie.

3. Spread the frosting on the cookie with a craft stick or plastic knife.

4. Add rainbow sprinkles to the cookie.

5. Add 2 or 3 drops of green food coloring to a cup of milk.

6. Use a straw to stir milk so that it magically turns green.

Caution: Be aware of children who may be allergic to milk.

Alternative: Substitute rice cakes for the sugar cookies, cream cheese for the white frosting, and sprouts for the sprinkles.

♫ I'm a Little Leprechaun

(Tune: "Mary Had a Little Lamb")

I'm a little leprechaun, leprechaun, leprechaun.
I'm a little leprechaun dressed in green.

At the end of a rainbow, a rainbow, a rainbow,
At the end of a rainbow, I hide my pot of gold.

If you ever catch me, catch me, catch me.
If you ever catch me, I'll give my gold to you.

St. Patrick's Day Stories

Jack and the Leprechaun
by Ivan Robertson
(Random House Books for Young Readers)

Leprechaun Gold
by Teresa Bateman (Holiday House)

Leprechauns Never Lie
by Lorna Balian (Star Bright Books)

Lucky O'Leprechaun
by Jana Dillon (Pelican Publishing Co.)

St. Patrick's Day
by Gail Gibbons (Holiday House)

St. Patrick's Day in the Morning
by Jan Brett (Clarion Books)

Three Cheers for March PreK–K, SV 9840-X

Leprechaun's Treasure

Materials

- patterns on page 51
- overhead projector
- pencil
- markers

- scissors
- gold or yellow paint
- paintbrushes
- stapler
- tape

- 6" thin paper plates
- photo of each child
- white and black poster board
- story from list on page 44

Directions

Teacher Preparation: Use the overhead projector to enlarge the patterns to desired size. Reproduce the leprechaun on white poster board and the pot on black. Cut them out. Color the leprechaun. Arrange and staple patterns on the bulletin board. Cut a circle the size of the photos from the center of each plate.

1. Listen to a story from the book list on page 44 about leprechauns and their gold.

2. Paint a paper plate gold or yellow to represent a coin. Allow it to dry.

3. Tape the photo to the back of the plate "picture frame."

4. Arrange and staple the "coins" to fill the pot on the bulletin board.

Three Cheers for March PreK–K, SV 9840-X

Saint Patrick's Day Centers

 **Sensory Center**

Math Standard
Compares groups and recognizes *more than*, *less than*, and *equal to*

Leprechaun Goop

Materials

- mixing bowl
- measuring cups
- 2 cups water
- plastic tablecloth
- spoon
- 6 cups cornstarch
- green food coloring

Teacher Preparation: Mix cornstarch, water, and several drops of green food coloring to form goop. Cover table with plastic cloth. Make measuring cups and a portion of goop available for each child.

Invite children to use the measuring cups and their hands to explore the goop. Challenge children to compare the amounts of goop in the measuring cups by using *more than*, *less than*, and *equal to*.

 **Math Center**

Math Standard
Reproduces simple patterns

Pattern Bracelets

Materials

- different kinds of green beads
- elastic cord
- index cards
- green plastic straws
- scissors
- empty butter tubs

Teacher Preparation: Cut the straws into one-inch pieces. Fill each butter tub with round beads, pony beads, and straw pieces. Cut the elastic cord in lengths long enough for a bracelet and tie a knot at one end of each length. Write several pattern starters, such as ABABAB, AABB, or ABBABB on index cards.

Have children choose one of the index cards. Then have them select two of the items in the tubs. Invite children to practice patterning skills by stringing the items on the elastic cord according to the card that was chosen. Tie the ends together to make the bracelet.

Saint Patrick's Day Centers

Math Standard
Applies and adapts a variety of appropriate strategies to solve problems

Puzzle Center

Pot of Gold Puzzle

Materials

- pattern on page 52
- poster board
- glue
- crayons or markers
- scissors

Teacher Preparation: Duplicate the pattern. Color and cut out the picture. Cut a piece of poster board to match the size of the picture. Glue the picture to the poster board and laminate for durability. Cut apart the picture on the lines indicated to make the puzzle.

Place the puzzle pieces on a table. Have children put the puzzle together.

Tip: Write a number from 1 to 12 on the back of each puzzle piece for children to use for self checking.

Science Standard
Understands light

Science Center

Prism Rainbows

Materials

- prism
- white paper
- water hose
- crayons
- picture of a rainbow

Teacher Preparation: Become familiar with what causes a rainbow. Light is made up of the colors in a rainbow. When white light shines through a raindrop or a prism, it is broken into a spectrum of colors. Each color comes through at a different angle and, therefore, allows the eye to see each separate color.

Take children outside on a sunny day and spray a water hose so that they can see the rainbow colors reflected. Place a prism near a window or other light source. Have children work with a partner. Challenge one child to turn the prism so that the rainbow colors appear on a paper. Then have the partner use the crayons to copy the prism reflections.

Saint Patrick's Day Centers

Language Center

Where Is the Leprechaun?

Materials

- booklet on pages 53 and 54
- sentence strips
- scissors
- crayons
- stapler
- black marker

Teacher Preparation: Duplicate a copy of the booklet for each child. Assemble the pages and staple. Cut apart sentence strips and write one of the following sight words on each card: *a*, *has*, *He*, *I*, *see*, *The*.

Introduce the sight words in the booklet using the word cards. Read the booklet to the children and have them follow along. When children are familiar with the words, place the booklets in the language center. Invite children to read and trace the words on each page and then draw a picture. For words such as *rainbow* and *leprechaun*, encourage them to use the beginning sound of the word as a clue.

Game Center

Fill the Pot of Gold

Materials

- round laundry basket
- black craft paper
- several yellow tennis balls
- masking tape
- bath towel

Teacher Preparation: Cover the laundry basket with black paper to resemble a pot. Fold the towel and place it in the bottom of the basket. The towel will prevent the balls from bouncing out of the basket. Place a piece of masking tape on the floor so that it is several feet from the basket.

Read a story from the book list on page 44 about leprechauns and their gold. Have children stand on the masking tape and toss a ball into the basket. Have them continue until all of the "gold" is in the pot.

Challenge volunteers to create a graph using pictures to show how much "gold" each student tosses into the "pot."

Saint Patrick's Day Centers

Art Center

Language Arts Standard
Writes own name correctly and legibly

Shamrock Collage

Materials

- shamrock pattern on page 50
- shallow pan
- 3 or 4 different fabrics which are mostly green
- water
- white construction paper
- black marker
- scissors
- glue

Teacher Preparation: Enlarge and cut out the shamrock pattern and trace the shape on the white construction paper. Provide a copy for each child. Cut a generous supply of fabric into one- or two-inch squares. Mix an equal amount of glue and water in the shallow pan.

Have children cut out the shamrock and write their name on the back. Then have them dip one square of fabric in the thinned glue and place it on the paper. Repeat the procedure until the shamrock is completely covered.

Writing Center

Language Arts Standard
Uses letters to represent words

What a Mess!

Materials

- activity master on page 55
- green tempera paint
- crayons or markers
- paintbrush
- pencil

Teacher Preparation: Before children arrive, paint tiny footprints on the tables and the floor. Then place any items in the room that are green in a pile on the floor. Include toys, books, papers, or crayons. Duplicate a copy of the activity master for each child.

When children enter the room, discuss with them who might have left the room in a mess. Lead to them to the conclusion that it was the leprechauns. Then have them go to the writing center and write or dictate a story telling why the leprechauns were in the room. Invite them to draw a picture of what the room looked like.

Shamrock Patterns

Use with "Wearing of the Green" on page 42 and with "Shamrock Collage" on page 49.

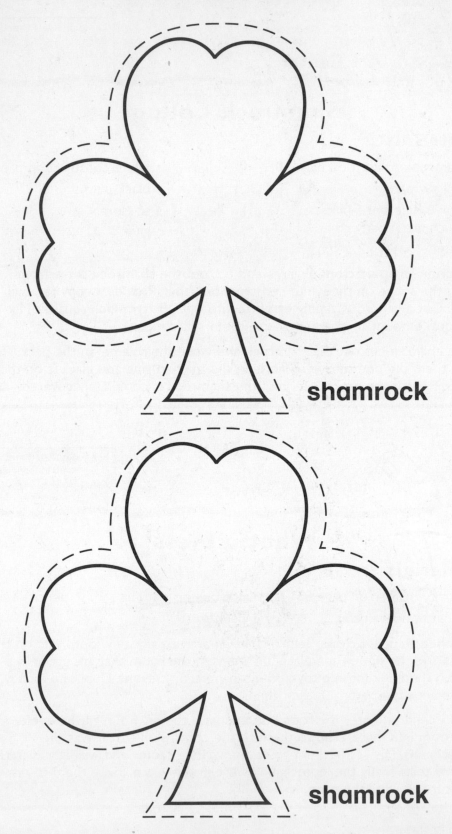

shamrock

shamrock

Three Cheers for March PreK–K, SV 9840-X

Leprechaun and Pot of Gold Patterns

Use with "Leprechaun's Treasure" on page 45.

Three Cheers for March PreK–K, SV 9840-X

Leprechaun Puzzle Pattern

Use with "Pot of Gold Puzzle" on page 47.

Unit 4, Saint Patrick's Day: Patterns
Three Cheers for March PreK–K, SV 9840-X

Booklet Pages
Use with "Where Is the Leprechaun?" on page 48.

I see a rainbow.

1

I see a leprechaun.

2

Three Cheers for March PreK–K, SV 9840-X

Booklet Pages (continued)

Use with "Where Is the Leprechaun?" on page 48.

He has a pot.

3

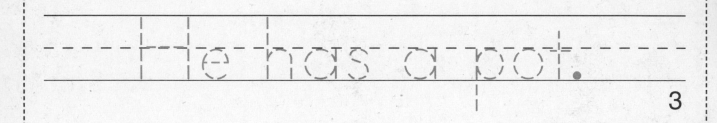

The pot has gold.

4

Name _____

Mystery Guests

The leprechauns came to our room to _____

_____

_____ .

Directions: Use with "What a Mess!" on page 49. Have children write or dictate a story telling why the leprechauns were in the room. Invite children to draw a picture of what the room looked like.

The Wild West

The first cowboys came from Mexico. The *vaqueros*, the Spanish word for cowboys, were men who rode horses and took care of cattle.

American people began to copy the vaqueros when they saw them move their cattle north into America to graze.

American cowboys developed special clothing that protected them from the harsh conditions associated with working cattle.

Cowboys wore wide-brimmed hats to hide their faces from the sun. They could also dip their hat into a running stream when they were thirsty.

Cowboys wore a bandana knotted around their neck so that they could use it to cover their nose and mouth to filter out the dust.

Cowboys wore leather chaps to protect their legs when they rode through the brush and cacti.

The high heels on their boots prevented their feet from slipping through the stirrups of their saddle.

One of the responsibilities of the cowboy was to take a herd of cattle to market in towns that were far away. These longs trips were called cattle drives.

In the mid-1800's, cowboys began challenging the bronc riding and roping skills of other cowboys. This was the beginning of the rodeo.

Clothespin Horse

Materials

- patterns on page 65
- brown, black, white construction paper
- black yarn
- spring-type clothespins (2 per child)
- small wiggly eyes
- crayons or markers
- scissors
- glue
- hole punch

Directions.

Teacher Preparation: Duplicate and cut out the patterns to form templates or duplicate the patterns on construction paper for younger children.

1. Trace the saddle on brown construction paper and cut it out.

2. Trace the horse on a desired color of construction paper and cut it out.

3. Use crayons or markers to draw markings on both sides of the horse.

4. Glue a wiggly eye on each side of the horse's head.

5. Use scissors to snip the mane on the horse's neck.

6. Fold the saddle and glue it in place.

7. Punch holes for the reins and the tail.

8. Loop yarn through the hole and tie ends together for the reins.

9. Loop several strings of yarn through the hole for the tail and tie.

10. Clip two clothespins on for the legs.

Pipe Cleaner Branding

Materials

- patterns on page 66
- brown construction paper
- white construction paper
- crayons
- scissors
- glue
- pipe cleaners
- black tempera paint

Directions.

Teacher Preparation: Duplicate and cut out the patterns to form templates. Bend pipe cleaners to create branding irons in the shape of letters. If possible, make the first letter of each child's name.

1. Trace the body and the head on brown construction paper.

2. Be creative and draw the cow's tail on the brown paper.

3. Trace two horns on a small piece of white construction paper.

4. Cut out all of the pieces.

5. Glue the horns on the head.

6. Glue the head and the tail on opposite ends of the body.

7. Draw the eyes, nostrils, and hooves with a black crayon.

8. Use a white crayon to draw curly white hair on the head and on the belly.

9. Dip the pipe cleaner "brand" in black paint and stamp it on the hip of the cow.

Three Cheers for March PreK–K, SV 9840-X

Cowhand Cookout

You will need

- 2 large cans of pork and beans
- 2 packages of hot dog wieners
- canned biscuits (one biscuit per child)
- electric cooking pot
- serving spoon
- plastic knives and spoons
- aluminum pie pans (one per child)
- plastic cups for water
- napkins
- items for a campfire
- flashlight
- cowboy music

Directions

Teacher Preparation: Bake biscuits ahead of time. Set up an area of the classroom with a campfire using a few logs with yellow, red, and orange tissue paper for the flames. Position the flashlight between the logs so that it will shine through the tissue paper to resemble fire. Place objects that children can sit on in a circle around the campfire. Use logs, blocks, tubs, or buckets turned upside down.

1. Pour pork and beans into cooking pot.

2. Cut hot dogs into small pieces and put them into the pot. Make sure that pieces are small enough to avoid choking. Stir and heat.

3. Sit around campfire and serve beans and wieners and the biscuits on aluminum pie plates.

4. Turn off classroom lights and eat by the light of the fire. Play cowboy music.

Three Cheers for March PreK–K, SV 9840-X

🎵 The Cowboy on the Range

(Tune: "Farmer in the Dell")

The cowboy wears a hat.

The cowboy wears a hat.

Yippee-ki-ay and howdy-do.

The cowboy wears a hat.

The cowboy wears a vest.

The cowboy wears a vest.

Yippee-ki-ay and howdy-do.

The cowboy wears a vest.

Choose one child to be the cowboy or cowgirl and have him or her put on the piece of clothing named in the song or role-play the actions in each verse. Add the following verses:

• wears a bandana
• wears two boots
• rides a horse
• ropes the cows

Cowboy Tales

Armadillo Rodeo
by Jan Brett (Scholastic)

Cindy Ellen: A Wild West Cinderella
by Susan Lowell (Joanna Cotler)

Cowboys
by Marie and Douglas Gorsline (Random House)

Little Red Cowboy Hat
by Susan Lowell (Henry Holt & Company, Inc.)

Pecos Bill
by Steven Kellogg (HarperTrophy)

The Cowboy and the Black-eyed Pea
by Tony Johnston (Puffin Publishers)

Way Out West with a Baby
by Michael Brownlow (Ragged Bear US)

Why Cowboys Sleep with Their Boots On
by Laurie Lazzaro Knowlton
(Pelican Publishing Co.)

Little Cowhands

Materials

- patterns on page 67
- construction paper (a variety of colors)
- red craft paper
- 9" thin paper plates
- wallpaper samples
- black, brown, orange, and yellow yarn
- scissors
- glue
- crayons or markers
- stapler

Directions

Teacher Preparation: Cover bulletin board with red craft paper. Enlarge the hat and bandana patterns to the size of the paper plate. Cut them out to form templates. Provide a generous supply of wallpaper samples for bandanas.

1. Draw a face on the paper plate.

2. Cut pieces of yarn that match your hair color and glue them above the face.

3. Trace the hat template on construction paper. Cut it out and glue it on the plate to cover the hair.

4. Choose a wallpaper sample and trace the bandana template on it. Cut out the bandana and glue it below the face.

5. Arrange and staple the faces on the bulletin board.

Three Cheers for March PreK–K, SV 9840-X

The Wild West Centers

Art Center

Decorative Bandanas

Materials

- masking tape
- unbleached muslin fabric
- several different tempera paint colors
- several different Western-theme sponges (cactus, star, horse)
- table
- scissors
- markers

Teacher Preparation: Cut fabric into 18" squares and then cut each square on the diagonal to form two triangle-shaped bandanas. Provide each child with a bandana.

Have children smooth the bandana and tape it to the table. Have them sponge-paint shapes on the fabric and use markers to add a decorative border. Allow the bandana to dry and tie it around children's necks. Challenge each child to describe his or her bandana.

Language Center

Where's My Hat?

Materials

- patterns on page 68
- crayons or markers
- file folder
- scissors
- library pocket
- glue

Teacher Preparation: Duplicate several copies of the patterns. Color and cut them out. Glue a library pocket to the outside of the file folder. Arrange and glue the cowboys on the inside of the file folder, leaving space for the hats. Write a capital letter on each hat and a partner letter on each cowboy's bandana. This game can also be used to match picture names with beginning sounds. Glue a picture on the hat and write the beginning sound of the picture's name on the bandana. Store hats in the library pocket.

Have children put the hat on the cowboy that has the matching partner letter.

The Wild West Centers

Language Arts Standard
Explores language as a variety of materials are read

Writing Center

A Very Tall Tale

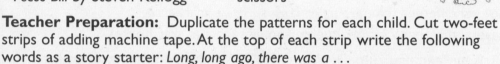

Materials

- patterns on page 69
- adding machine tape
- *Pecos Bill* by Steven Kellogg
- pencil
- crayons or markers
- scissors

Teacher Preparation: Duplicate the patterns for each child. Cut two-feet strips of adding machine tape. At the top of each strip write the following words as a story starter: *Long, long ago, there was a . . .*

Read *Pecos Bill* and discuss with children the meaning of a tall tale. Have children color and cut out the top and bottom of the horse. Then have them dictate a tall tale using the story starter. Some children will have a short, simple story while others will get excited over how "tall" they can make their story. Write each child's story on the adding machine tape and cut off any section of the strip that is not used. Glue the horse at the top and the bottom of the strip. Display for everyone to enjoy.

Math Standard
Uses familiar manipulatives to recognize shapes and their relationships

Block Center

Home on the Range

Materials

- plastic fences
- wooden blocks
- black markers
- toy horses and cows
- scissors
- pictures of cowboys working with cattle
- 1 or 2 small shoe boxes that have been painted brown

Teacher Preparation: Place materials in the block center. Display pictures on the wall.

Discuss with children the characteristics of a ranch. Introduce vocabulary words such as *fence, corral, bunkhouse,* and *range.* Invite children to use a marker and scissors to make a bunkhouse out of the shoe box. Then have them build a corral for the animals using the blocks. Invite children to role-play life on a ranch.

The Wild West Centers

Math Center

Math Standard
Understands the meaning
of addition and subtraction

Roundup Game

Materials

- pattern on page 70
- white construction paper
- one regular die
- one blank die
- 20 tiny plastic cows
- black sharp-tip marker
- one sheet of green construction paper

Teacher Preparation: Duplicate two copies of the corral on the white construction paper. Draw three + signs and three − signs on the sides of the blank die. Familiarize children with the terms *corral* and *range*.

Discuss with children the concept of adding and taking away. Then introduce the + and − signs. Have partners sit facing each other with a corral in front of each person. Place the green construction paper between the corrals to resemble the grass on the range. Place all of the plastic cows on the green paper. Have each partner take a turn rolling the two dice. If a + sign is shown, the child adds the designated number of cows to his or her corral. If a − sign is shown, the child takes away the designated number of cows and puts them back on the range. Players will skip a turn if the corral is empty. Play continues until all of the cows are in the corrals. The partner with the most cows wins the game.

Tip: If plastic cows are not available, use brown plastic snapping cubes.

www.harcourtschoolsupply.com
63
Unit 5, The Wild West: Centers
Three Cheers for March PreK–K, SV 9840-X

The Wild West Centers

Game Center

Language Arts Standard
Shares personal narrative through show and tell

Barrel Relay Race

Materials

- two stick horses
- two cowboy hats with chin strings
- two plastic trash cans (any size)

Teacher Preparation: Set the trash cans in a large open space.

Divide the class into two teams. Line up each team opposite a trash can. Give the first person in each line a hat and a stick horse. Have each child ride the stick horse around the "barrel" and return to the line. Each child then gives the hat and the horse to the next person who repeats the activity. Have children yell "Yippee-ki-ay" when everyone has had a turn.

Challenge volunteers from each team to describe the race.

Science Center

Science Standard
Understands organisms and their environments

Exploring Wildlife

Materials

- cactus
- snakeskins
- tumbleweeds
- wildflowers
- magnifying glass
- horns from cattle
- books about armadillos, roadrunners, coyotes, jack rabbits, and rattlesnakes

Teacher Preparation: Display any available items and books in the science center.

Have children use a magnifying glass to examine the objects in the center. Have them look at the pictures in the books to learn about the wildlife that cowhands might see.

Horse and Saddle Patterns

Use with "Clothespin Horse" on page 57.

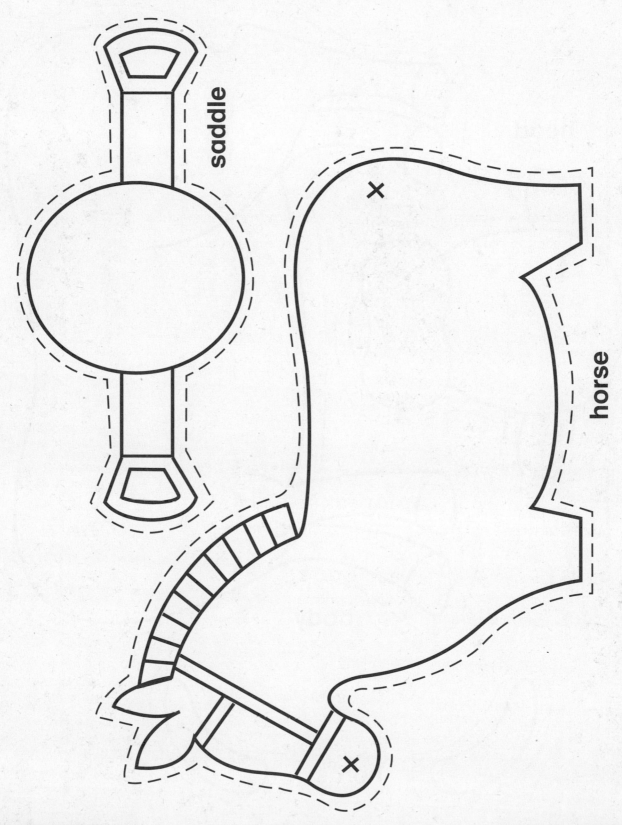

saddle

horse

Three Cheers for March PreK–K, SV 9840-X

Cow Patterns

Use with "Pipe Cleaner Branding" on page 57.

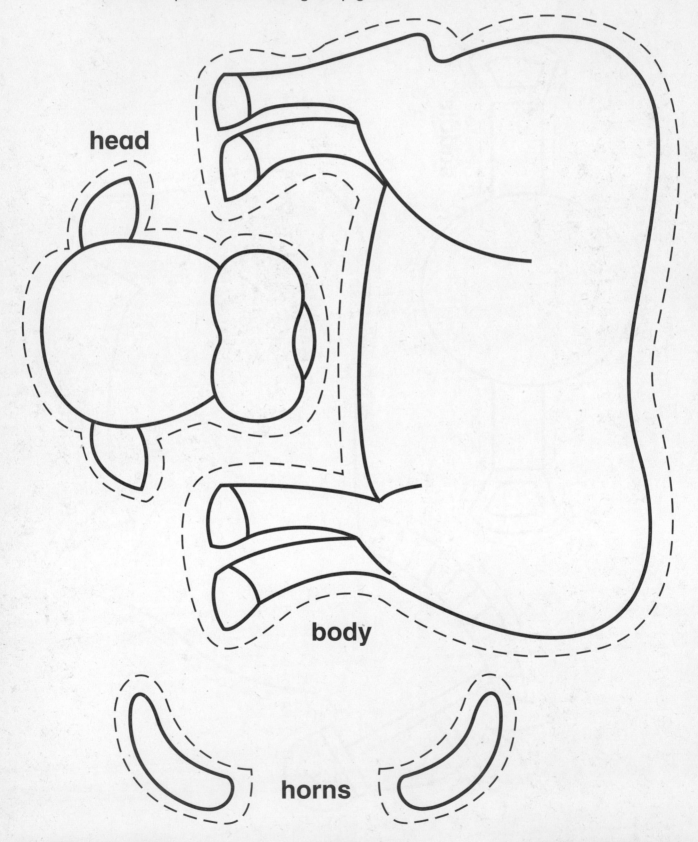

head

body

horns

Three Cheers for March PreK–K, SV 9840-X

Hat and Bandana Patterns

Use with "Little Cowhands" on page 60.

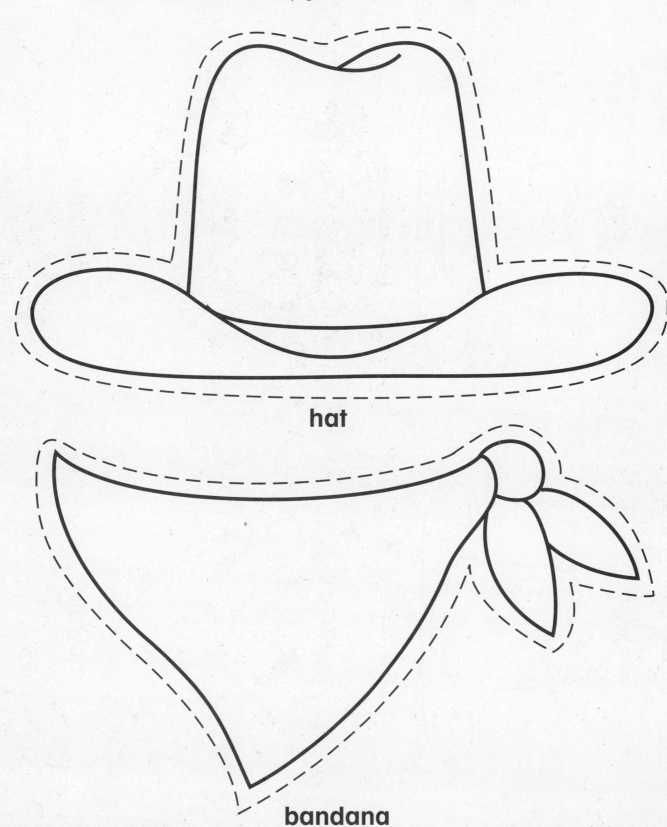

hat

bandana

Three Cheers for March PreK–K, SV 9840-X

Cowboy and Hat Patterns

Use with "Where's My Hat?" on page 61.

hat

cowboy

hat

cowboy

Unit 5, The Wild West: Patterns
Three Cheers for March PreK–K, SV 9840-X

Tall Tale Patterns

Use with "A Very Tall Tale" on page 62.

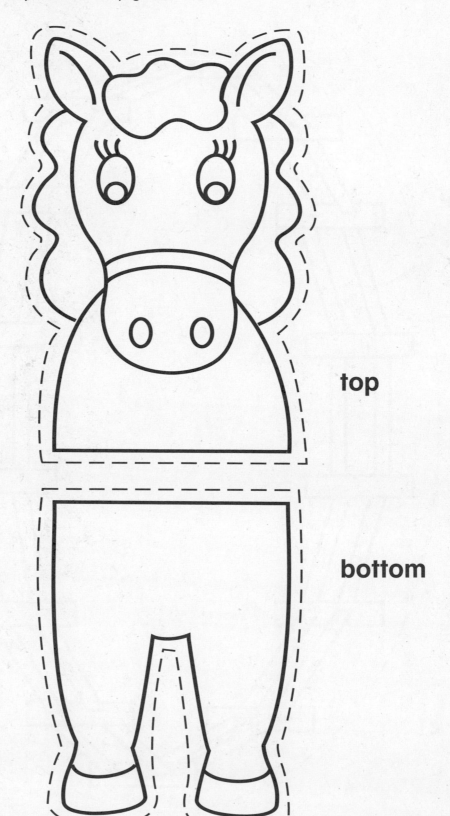

top

bottom

Corral Pattern

Use with "Roundup Game" on page 63.

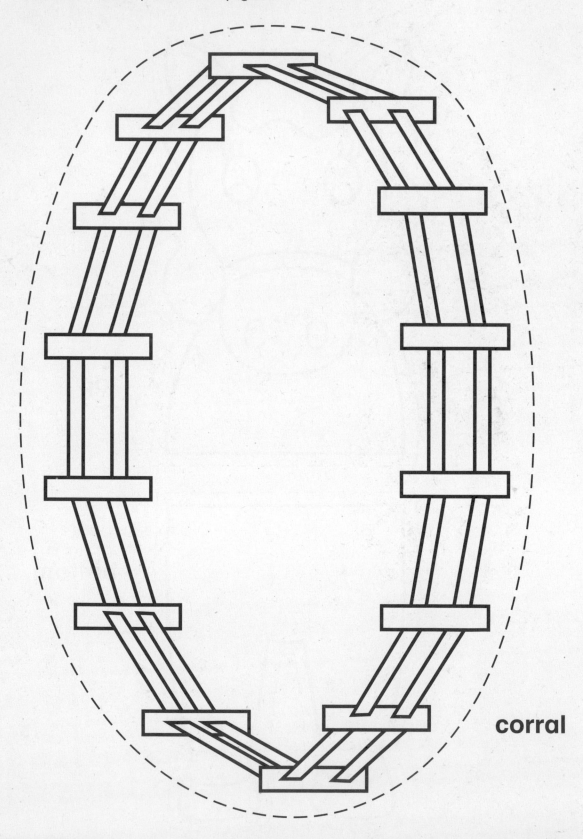

corral

Three Cheers for March PreK–K, SV 9840-X

Eating Healthy Foods

 The US Department of Agriculture (USDA) introduced the Food Guide Pyramid in 1992 as a guide for a healthy diet.

 Based on recent research, the Food Guide Pyramid is currently under revision. Check the USDA website for updated information.

 The Food Guide Pyramid suggests eating the recommended amounts from all of the food groups on a daily basis.

 Bread, cereal, rice, and pasta form a group of foods that provide vitamins, energy, and fiber needed for strong and healthy bodies.

 A variety of fruits and vegetables provide the necessary vitamins and minerals needed for healthy bodies.

 The main nutrient the body gets from the milk, yogurt, and cheese group is calcium. Calcium is essential for developing strong bones and teeth.

 Healthy bodies need protein and iron, which can be provided by lean meats, poultry, fish, dry beans, eggs, and nuts.

 Fats are necessary for the body to create cell membranes and hormones and for the growth and functioning of vital organs.

 Obesity is becoming a major health concern in the United States.

 In addition to eating healthy foods, daily exercise is also important for good health.

Three Cheers for March PreK–K, SV 9840-X

A Healthy Lunch

Materials

- *Lunch* by Denise Fleming
- brown lunch sacks
- manila paper
- crayons
- scissors
- poster of the food pyramid

Directions

Teacher Preparation: Display the food pyramid for children to see.

Read *Lunch* and discuss with children the foods that were included in the story. Help children identify which group each one belongs in according to the food pyramid.

1. Draw pictures of favorite foods that would make a healthy lunch.
2. Cut out the pictures and put them in the lunch sack.
3. Write the word *Lunch* on the bag.

A Good Foods Headband

Materials

- patterns on page 80
- sentence strips
- crayons
- scissors
- glue
- stapler

Directions

Teacher Preparation: Provide a copy of the patterns for each child.

Discuss with children the importance of eating foods from the different food groups. See the Teacher Information page for information about the food groups.

1. Cut out the circles and draw a picture of a food from each group on each circle.
2. Glue the circles on the sentence strip.
3. Wrap the sentence strip around the child's head and staple the ends to form a headband.

Three Cheers for March PreK–K, SV 9840-X

 # A Healthy Snack

You will need

- whole wheat bread (one slice per child)
- creamy peanut butter or cream cheese
- carrot sticks
- salad dressing
- vanilla yogurt (½ cup per child)
- fresh strawberries (washed and stems removed)
- bananas
- paper plates
- 6-ounce paper cups
- napkins
- plastic knives and spoons
- mixing bowl
- food pyramid poster

Directions

Teacher Preparation: Cut bread slices diagonally. Assemble items in an area so that children can help with preparation.

Discuss with children the importance of eating healthy foods. Have them locate each of the foods listed in the ingredients on the food pyramid.

1. Slice the strawberries and bananas into small pieces.

2. Pour yogurt into a mixing bowl and stir in the fruit until thoroughly mixed.

3. On a paper plate, give each child two halves of wheat bread and a dab of peanut butter or cream cheese. Have children spread the peanut butter or cream cheese on the bread and make a sandwich.

4. Give each child some carrot sticks and a small amount of salad dressing.

5. Fill a paper cup with yogurt and fruit for each child.

6. Enjoy these healthy snacks!

Tip: This activity can also be used to teach fractions and halves. Demonstrate by cutting the fruit into two equal parts before cutting it into smaller pieces.

Note: Be aware of children who may have food allergies.

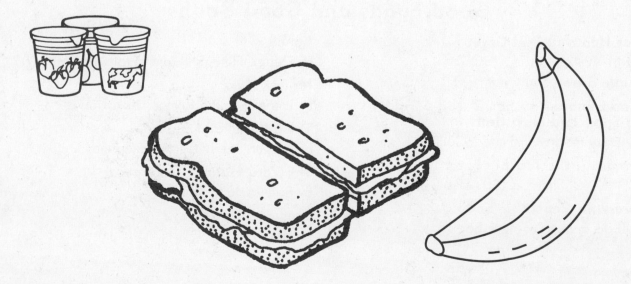

Three Cheers for March PreK–K, SV 9840-X

♫ Pizza Pokey

(Tune: "Hokey Pokey")

Have children stand in a circle around a large circle cutout of a pizza crust. Pass out to each child one paper cutout of an ingredient for the pizza. Have children lay the ingredient on the pizza crust when it is named.

Put the pepperoni in. Put the pepperoni out.

Put the pepperoni in and mix it all about.

Do the pizza-pokey and turn yourself around.

That's what it's all about! (Clap! Clap!)

Put the cheese in. Put the cheese out.

Put the cheese in and mix it all about.

Do the pizza-pokey and turn yourself around.

That's what it's all about! (Clap! Clap!)

Repeat verses with tomato, ham, sausage, mushrooms, and other pizza toppings.

Good Foods and Good Books

Eat Healthy, Feel Great
by M. William Sears
(Little Brown and Company)

Good Enough to Eat: A Kid's Guide to Food and Nutrition
by Lizzy Rockwell (HarperCollins)

Gregory, the Terrible Eater
by Mitchell Sharmat (Scholastic)

Growing Vegetable Soup
by Lois Ehlert (Voyager Books)

Lunch
by Denise Fleming (Henry Holt & Company)

Mouse Mess
by Linnea Asplind Riley (Scholastic)

The Edible Food Pyramid
by Loreen Leedy (Scott Foresman)

The Very Hungry Caterpillar
by Eric Carle (Scholastic)

Tops and Bottoms
by Janet Stevens (Harcourt Children's Books)

All Aboard the Healthy Foods Train

Materials

- blue craft paper
- patterns on page 81
- crayons or markers
- scissors
- stapler
- tempera paints
- paintbrushes
- white construction paper

Directions

Teacher Preparation: Cover the bulletin board with craft paper and enlarge the train pattern to desired size. Color and cut out the train cars (1 engine, 5 boxcars) and staple to the bulletin board in a pleasing arrangement. Label each car with a food group name.

Discuss with children the food groups that provide healthy food choices.

1. Paint a picture of a food that is healthy.

2. Allow pictures to dry and cut them out.

3. Staple the pictures on the appropriate train car.

Encourage children to choose different foods so that no food is repeated. There should be at least one picture for each food group.

Eating Healthy Foods Centers

Art Center

Math Standard
Reproduces simple patterns involving color and shape

Food Prints

Materials

- tempera paints (3 or 4 colors)
- 9" x 12" white construction paper
- a few raw fruits such as an apple or an orange
- a few raw vegetables such as a green pepper or a potato
- paper towels
- hand towels
- masking tape

Teacher Preparation: Cut fruits and vegetables horizontally across the middle into two sections. Make cuts as straight as possible. For each color of paint, fold two paper towels in half to make four thicknesses and fold a hand towel into fourths. Lay the folded paper towels on the hand towel and secure with tape. Cover the paper towel with a small amount of paint.

Have children dip the cut section of a fruit or vegetable into the paint, making sure that it is thoroughly covered. Then have them press it onto the construction paper to make a print. Repeat the procedure with other fruits and vegetables. Challenge children to reproduce the pattern made by another child.

Writing Center

Language Arts Standard
Uses letters to represent words

Writing a Food List

Materials

- activity master on page 85
- pencils

Teacher Preparation: Duplicate a copy of the activity master for each child.

Discuss with children the difference between healthy and unhealthy foods. Have children write or dictate a list of their five favorite healthy foods. Encourage older children to say the name of the food and write the sounds that they hear to promote independent writing.

Eating Healthy Foods Centers

Game Center

Math Standard
Demonstrates awareness of addition

Fishing for Good Foods

Materials

- pictures of healthy foods
- a large food pyramid poster
- container of interlocking cubes
- fishing pole with a magnet attached
- scissors
- paper clips
- black marker
- tape

Teacher Preparation: On each section of the food pyramid write a number from 1 to 4, repeating numbers as needed. Make the numbers visible to children. Place a paper clip on each food picture.

Spread the food pictures out on the floor next to the food pyramid. Have children take turns "catching" a food picture with the fishing pole. Then challenge them to tape the picture on the correct section of the food pyramid. Have them identify the number written in that section and snap together that many interlocking cubes. Children will add cubes to their stack with each turn. When all of the food pictures have been placed on the pyramid, have children count up their "points."

Language Center

Language Arts Standard
Recognizes uppercase and lowercase letters

Letter Soup

Materials

- scissors
- library pocket
- patterns on page 82
- file folder
- crayons
- glue

Teacher Preparation: Duplicate five copies of the patterns. Color and cut out the five pots and five sets of food cards. Arrange and glue the pots on the inside of the file folder. Then write a letter on each of the pots. On the back of each set of food cards, write the partner letter. Have children put the vegetables in the pots by matching the partner letters.

Eating Healthy Foods Centers

Math Center

Math Standard
Uses a number line up to 100

Estimating Vegetables

Materials

- pencil
- chart tablet
- number line to 100
- bushel basket filled with potatoes (or other vegetable)

Teacher Preparation: Hang the number line on the wall near the math center. Write "How Many Potatoes Are in the Basket?" at the top of the chart tablet.

Have children write their name on the chart tablet. Then have them estimate how many potatoes are in the basket and write that number next to their name. Challenge them to find the number that they guessed and circle it on the number line. When all children have visited the center and recorded their guesses, have them sit in a circle with the basket in the middle. Tell them that they are going to count the potatoes to find out whose guess is the closest to the real amount. Invite children to make piles of ten potatoes in each pile until the basket is empty. Then count by tens to find the total number of potatoes. Circle the number on the number line. Refer to the chart tablet and find the child whose guess was the closest to the actual number. For younger children, use a smaller basket with no more than twenty potatoes.

Eating Healthy Foods Centers

 **Reading Center**

Language Arts Standard
Sequences events accurately

Parts of a Story

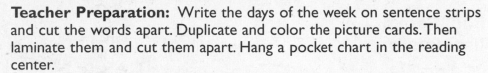

Materials

- marker
- sentence strips
- *The Very Hungry Caterpillar* by Eric Carle
- pocket chart
- picture cards on pages 83 and 84

Teacher Preparation: Write the days of the week on sentence strips and cut the words apart. Duplicate and color the picture cards. Then laminate them and cut them apart. Hang a pocket chart in the reading center.

Read *The Very Hungry Caterpillar*. Have children retell the story by putting the days of the week cards in the pocket chart beginning with Monday. Then have them place the picture of the food that the caterpillar ate next to the day of the week on which he ate it. Or, have children sort the picture cards in groups of healthy and unhealthy foods.

 **Dramatic Play Center**

Math Standard
Knows the value of a penny, nickel, and dime

Good Health Restaurant

Materials

- poster of the food pyramid
- cash register, real coins (pennies, nickels, dimes)
- empty containers, pictures, or plastic pieces of healthy foods
- dress up items for a waitperson such as aprons, order pads, or hats

Teacher Preparation: Provide a generous supply of healthy food choices in the center. Display the food pyramid poster. Make a menu with pictures of the food choices and prices.

Have children role-play going to a restaurant and ordering a healthy meal. Challenge them to refer to the food pyramid and select an item from each section. Provide children with real coins so that they can count the correct amount when they "pay" for their meal.

Circle Patterns

Use with "A Good Foods Headband" on page 72.

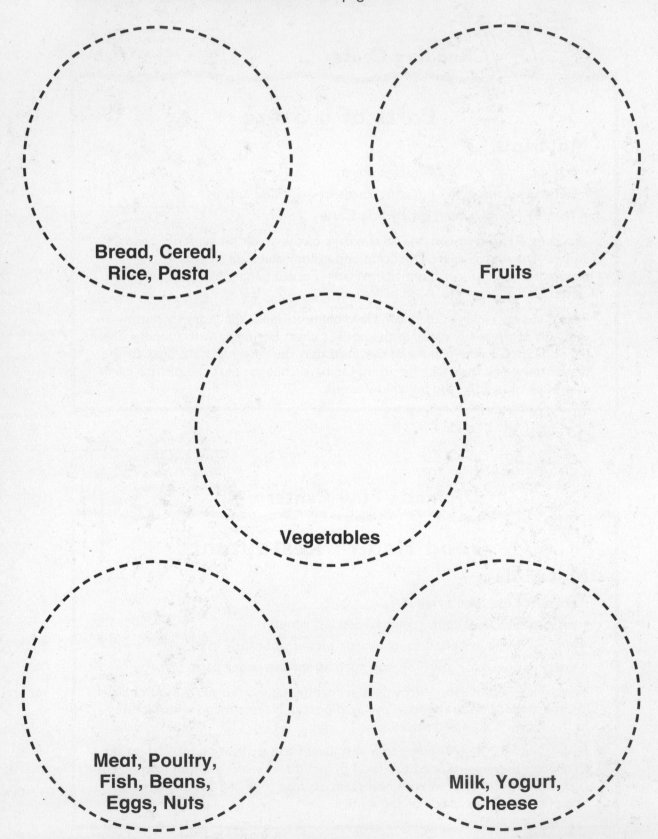

Bread, Cereal, Rice, Pasta

Fruits

Vegetables

Meat, Poultry, Fish, Beans, Eggs, Nuts

Milk, Yogurt, Cheese

Train Pattern

Use with "All Aboard the Healthy Foods Train" on page 75.

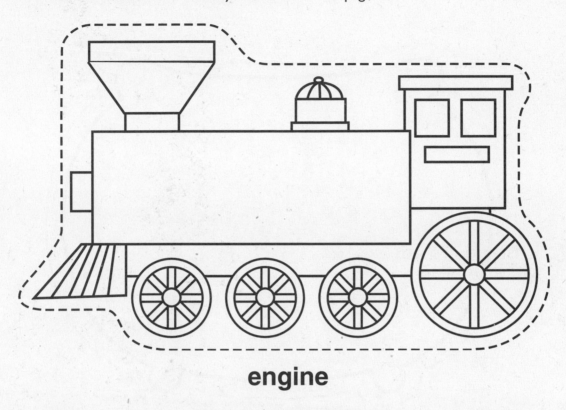

engine

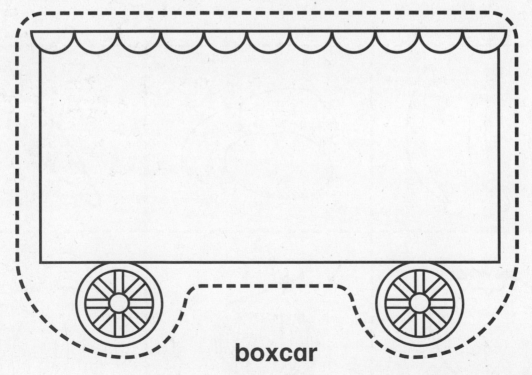

boxcar

Three Cheers for March PreK–K, SV 9840-X

Pot and Food Card Patterns

Use with "Letter Soup" on page 77.

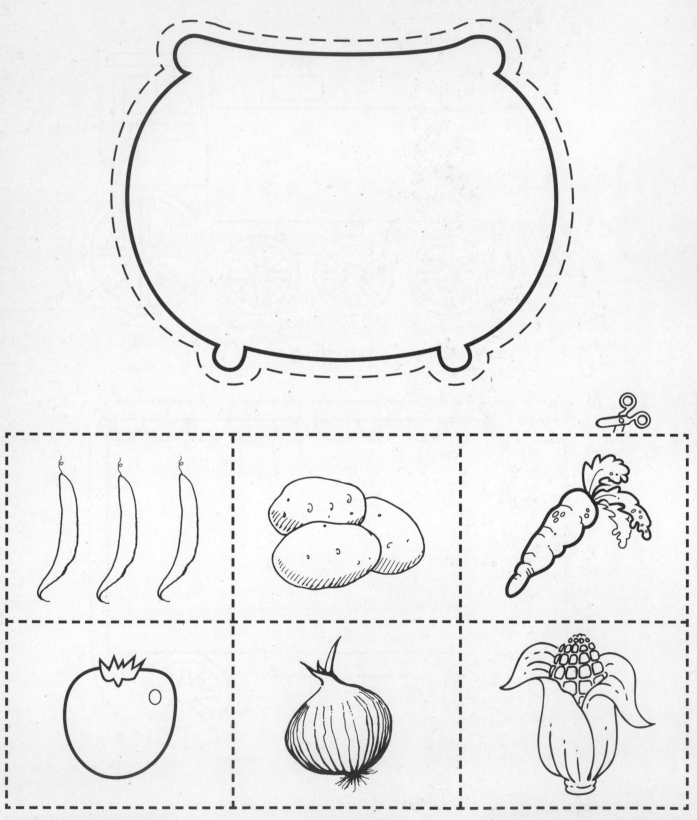

Food Picture Cards

Use with "Parts of a Story" on page 79.

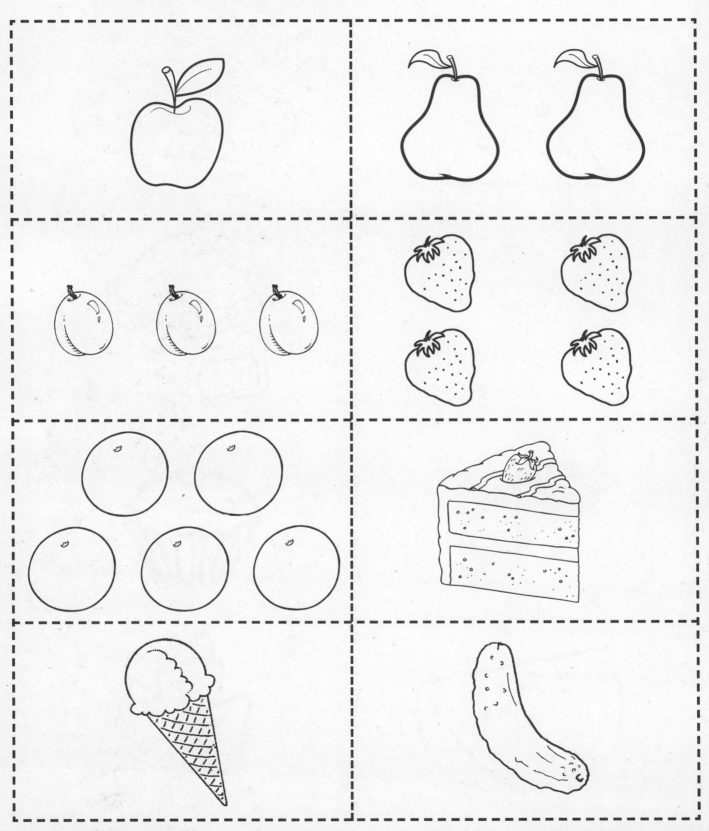

Food Picture Cards (continued)

Use with "Parts of a Story" on page 79.

Unit 6, Eating Healthy Foods: Cards
Three Cheers for March PreK–K, SV 9840-X

Name _____

Food List

My favorite healthy foods are:

1. _____

2. _____

3. _____

4. _____

5. _____

Directions: Use with "Writing a Food List" on page 76. Have children write or dictate a list of their five favorite healthy foods.

Unit 6, Eating Healthy Foods: Activity Master
Three Cheers for March PreK–K, SV 9840-X

A Look at Dr. Seuss

(Theodor Geisel, Theo LeSieg)

 Theodor Seuss Geisel, better know as Dr. Seuss, was born on March 2, 1904, in Springfield, Massachusetts.

 He credited his mother with both his ability and desire to create rhymes because she often "chanted" rhymes to him when he was young.

 In 1937 he wrote his first book, *And to Think That I Saw It on Mulberry Street*, under the pen name of Dr. Seuss. Seuss was his middle name, and he put Dr. in front of it because his father had always wanted him to be a doctor.

 In 1957 he was approached by the Houghton Mifflin Publishing Company to write a book that would excite beginning readers. He took the 220 words on the current reading list and created *The Cat in the Hat*. It was an instant success.

 He and his wife then began the Beginner Books of Random House. At times he wrote under the name of Theo LeSieg (Geisel spelled backwards) and let others illustrate the books. Sometimes other authors and illustrators did the books. All of the books used approved educational word lists.

 Bennet Cerf, a TV personality in 1960, bet Geisel $50 that he could not write an entire book using only fifty words. Geisel wrote *Green Eggs and Ham* as a result of that bet.

 Theodor Seuss Geisel died September 24, 1991, in California.

 In 1998 the National Education Association started the Read Across America event to get children excited about reading. The yearlong program culminates every year on Dr. Seuss's birthday.

Unit 7, Author Study: Teacher Information
Three Cheers for March PreK–K, SV 9840-X

Literature Selection:
The Cat in the Hat by Dr. Seuss

In honor of Dr. Seuss's birthday and the National Read Across America Program on March 2, read *The Cat in the Hat*. Have children listen for words that rhyme. Then select a few words from the book and write them on the chalkboard. Challenge children to make a list of words that rhyme with the selected words.

A "Cat in the Hat" Hat

Materials

- 12" x 18" white construction paper (one per child)
- 9" thin paper plate (one per child)
- red tempera paint
- paintbrushes
- black watercolor paint
- scissors
- stapler

Directions

Teacher Preparation: Cut out the inner section of each paper plate and discard. Use the remaining outside edge to make the rim of the hat. Provide an outside rim for each child.

1. Paint wide red stripes across the length of the construction paper. Allow paint to dry.

2. Bring together the two short sides of the painted construction paper by overlapping one side on top of the other. Staple the sides together to make a cylinder.

3. Make two-inch cuts along the bottom edge of the entire cylinder to form tabs.

4. Fold the tabs out and slide the paper plate rim over the cylinder so that it sits on the tabs.

5. Staple the rim to the tabs to form the hat.

6. Paint the tip of each child's nose with black watercolor paint and add whiskers to resemble a cat.

Rhyme Time

Materials

- activity master on page 90
- scissors
- glue
- crayons

Directions

Teacher Preparation: Duplicate a copy of the activity master for each child.

Have children cut out the pictures and glue them next to the pictures that rhyme.

Rainy Day Fun

Materials

- activity master on page 91
- crayons or markers
- pencils

Directions

Teacher Preparation: Duplicate a copy of the activity master for each child.

Have children dictate or write what they would do on a rainy day and then draw a picture.

Books by Dr. Seuss

(Theodor Geisel, Theo LeSieg)

- *And to Think That I Saw It on Mulberry Street* (Random House)

- *Fox in Socks* (Random House)

- *Green Eggs and Ham* (Random House)

- *Horton Hatches the Egg* (Random House)

- *Horton Hears a Who* (Random House)

- *Hop on Pop* (Random House)

- *How the Grinch Stole Christmas* (Random House)

- *If I Ran the Circus* (Random House)

- *If I Ran the Zoo* (Random House)

- *Ten Apples Up on Top* by Theo LeSieg (Random House)

- *The Cat in the Hat* (Random House)

- *The Cat in the Hat Comes Back* (Random House)

- *The Lorax* (Random House)

- *Oh, the Places You'll Go* (Random House)

- *One Fish Two Fish Red Fish Blue Fish* (Random House)

- *Wacky Wednesday* (Random House)

- *Yertle the Turtle* (Random House)

For more information visit the website www.seussville.com.

Bookmark Patterns

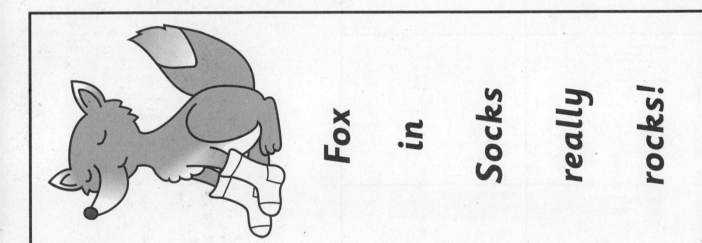

Let's read about that Cat in the Hat!

Fox in Socks really rocks!

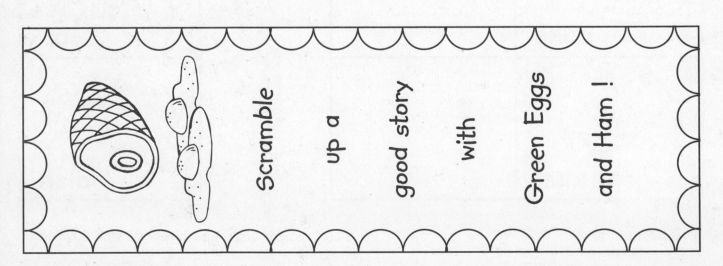

Scramble up a good story with Green Eggs and Ham!

Unit 7, Author Study: Patterns
Three Cheers for March PreK–K, SV 9840-X

Name _____

Rhyming

hat

bow

fish

cake

kite

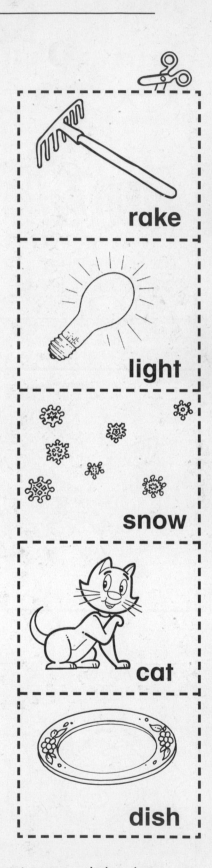

rake

light

snow

cat

dish

Directions: Use with "Rhyme Time" on page 87. Have children cut out the pictures and glue them next to the pictures that rhyme.

Unit 7, Author Study: Activity Master
Three Cheers for March PreK–K, SV 9840-X

Name _____

Rainy Day Writing

On a rainy day, I would _____ .

Directions: Use with "Rainy Day Fun" on page 87. Have children dictate or write what they would do on a rainy day and then draw a picture.

Unit 7, Author Study: Activity Master
Three Cheers for March PreK–K, SV 9840-X

Center Icons Patterns

Art Center

Block Center

Dramatic Play Center

Game Center

Center Icons Patterns
Three Cheers for March PreK–K, SV 9840-X

Center Icons Patterns

Language Center

Math Center

Music Center

Puzzle Center

Three Cheers for March PreK–K, SV 9840-X

Center Icons Patterns

Reading Center

Science Center

Sensory Center

Writing Center

Student Awards

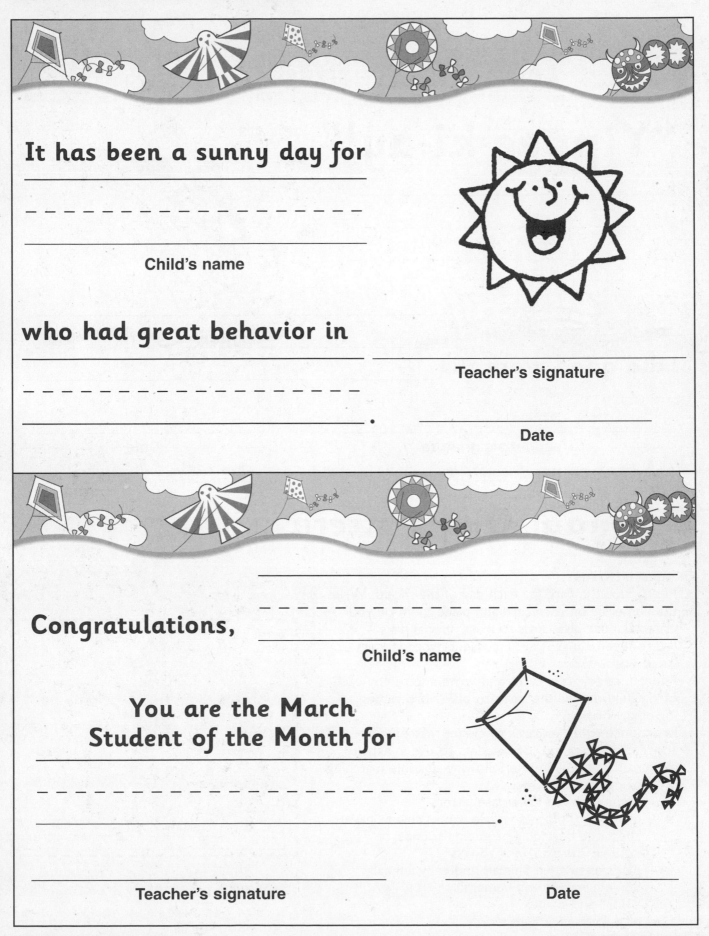

It has been a sunny day for

_____

- - - - - - - - - - - - - -

Child's name

who had great behavior in

_____

- - - - - - - - - - - - - -

_____ .

Teacher's signature

_____

Date

_____

- - - - - - - - - - - - - -

Child's name

Congratulations,

You are the March
Student of the Month for

_____

- - - - - - - - - - - - - -

_____ .

_____

Teacher's signature

_____

Date

Student Awards Patterns
Three Cheers for March PreK–K, SV 9840-X

Student Awards

"Yippee-ki-ay!"

_____

- -

_____

Child's name

_____

did good work in - .

_____

Teacher's signature   **Date**

Calendar Day Pattern

Suggested Uses

- Reproduce the card for each day of the month. Write the numerals on each card and place them on your class calendar. Use cards to mark special days.
- Reproduce to make cards to use in word ladders or word walls.
- Reproduce to make cards and write a letter on each card. Children use the cards to play word games forming words.
- Reproduce to make cards to create matching or concentration games for students to use in activity centers. Choose from the following possible matching skills or create your own:
    - uppercase and lowercase letters
    - pictures of objects whose names rhyme, have the same beginning or ending sounds, or contain short or long vowels
    - pictures of adult animals and baby animals
    - number words and numerals
    - colors and shapes
    - high-frequency sight words